Daily Reflections for Personal Growth

Book 1: Autumn – Transformative Reflections

Ken P. S. de Guzman

E-book ISBN: 978-981-18-7826-8
Paperback ISBN: 978-981-18-7863-3

DEDICATION

To all seekers on the path of the mind,
This book is for you, one of a kind.
For inner growth, wisdom you'll find,
In these pages, may your spirit unwind.

Próximamente...

El amor que vino de la quinta dimensión.
Pininos del estado del sueño.
Aproximación a la concentración.
El Shiatsu que yo aprendí.
El toque criollo.
Conversaciones con los seres vegetales.
Historia escrita.
Los 40 jinetes de la sanación.

Información de contacto

Correo:

domingo.alberto.montes@gmail.com

Facebook:

https://www.facebook.com/profile.php?id=1081942890

Twitter:

http://twitter.com/EigyoMontes

Sígueme en Instagram:

https://www.instagram.com/eigyo.montes/

eBooks:

https://books2read.com/ap/nl0B6b/Domingo-A-Montes-G

Don't miss out!

Visit the website below and you can sign up to receive emails whenever Domingo A. Montes G. publishes a new book. There's no charge and no obligation.

https://books2read.com/r/B-A-AXBOB-OEELD

BOOKS 2 READ

Connecting independent readers to independent writers.

Also by Domingo A. Montes G.

Clásicos del Reiki Japonés
Usui Reiki Hikkei, Guía de Reiki de Usui Sensei

Miyamoto Musashi, Obras
Go Rin no Sho - El Libro de los Cinco Anillos

SHInTao Seichem Reiki - El estilo del Dragón de Fuego
SHInTao Seichem Reiki Shoden - Guia del Nivel Uno. El Sendero del
Dragón de Fuego.

Standalone
El Amado Arcángel Cassiel, Señor del rayo Oro/Violeta
El Néctar de las Divinas Enseñanzas - Meditación en los Divinos
Atributos
Sanación Espiritual con Péndulo Consagrado 'Nuestro Método', la
forma de péndulo más evolucionada
El sentido De La Vida - En castellano
El Abrazo Divino, el Tetra Yoga de Jesús el Cristo

Siete Capas
101 Preguntas, mitos y errores En la sanación espiritual
Bendiciones Para Todos

CONTENTS

ACKNOWLEDGMENTS

With deepest gratitude, we extend our praise,
To the philosophers who've lit wisdom's blaze.
To Socrates, Plato, and Aristotle's kin,
Your timeless teachings forever live within.

To Confucius, Lao Tzu, and the Tao's embrace,
Your insights guide us to find our rightful place.
To Descartes, Kant, and their thoughts profound,
We acknowledge the intellect you have crowned.

To Nietzsche, Sartre, and existential thought,
You've challenged us to question, to seek what's sought.
To Rousseau, Locke, and social contract's reign,
Your philosophies echo in our collective domain.

To Buddha, Gandhi, and the path of peace,
Your compassion and love will never cease.
To Emerson, Thoreau, and nature's grandeur,
We honor your wisdom that forever endures.

To all the philosophers, near and far,
Your words of wisdom have shaped who we are.
In this humble book, your teachings combine,
We acknowledge you all with reverence and rhyme.

INTRODUCTION: TRANSFORMATIVE REFLECTIONS IN AUTUMN'S EMBRACE

Welcome to the first book of our series, "Daily Reflections for Personal Growth - Book 1 Autumn: Transformative Reflections." Within these pages, we embark on a journey through the transformative months of September, October, and November, immersing ourselves in the richness of autumn's embrace and exploring the profound themes of legacy, connection, nurturing the mind, and cultivating gratitude and resilience.

September invites us to reflect on legacy and connection. As the warmth of summer begins to fade, we contemplate the impact we leave on the world and the relationships that shape our lives. Through daily reflections and contemplation, we explore the legacy we wish to create and the meaningful connections we seek to nurture. This month encourages us to ponder our values, the mark we want to make, and the profound interconnectedness of all beings.

In October, we delve into the art of nurturing the mind. As the days grow shorter and nature prepares for a season of transformation, we are encouraged to turn inward and cultivate the fertile soil of our thoughts. Through daily teachings and reflections, we explore the wisdom of great minds, ancient and contemporary, nurturing the garden of our minds and expanding our intellectual horizons. This month is a journey of self-discovery and mental nourishment.

November brings with it the themes of gratitude and resilience. As autumn leaves fall gracefully, we are reminded to find gratitude for life's blessings and foster resilience in the face of challenges. Through daily gratitude practices and introspection, we embark on a transformative journey of cultivating appreciation for the present moment, embracing resilience, and discovering the strength to overcome obstacles. This month invites us to tap into the power of gratitude and resilience to enhance our well-being and navigate life's ups and downs.

This book serves as a guide for embracing the transformative power of autumn. It offers a sanctuary of contemplation and growth, where each daily reflection invites you to delve deeper into your thoughts, emotions, and aspirations. It is an invitation to embrace the richness of autumn's embrace and discover the transformative potential within.

As you engage with the daily reflections and practices within these pages, may you find inspiration in the changing colors of the season, solace in the embrace of autumn's stillness, and wisdom in the transformative power of introspection. May this journey through autumn awaken your inner strength, foster personal growth, and lead you towards a more authentic and fulfilling life.

Now, let us embark on this transformative autumn voyage together, as we explore the treasures of daily reflections and embrace the beauty of personal growth. Through the changing landscapes and introspective exercises, may you discover profound insights, cultivate resilience, and emerge with a renewed sense of self-awareness and purpose.

Embrace the essence of autumn's transformative reflections, for within them lies the potential for profound personal growth. Let us embark on this journey of self-discovery and transformation, guided by the daily reflections that await us in the pages ahead.

SEPTEMBER – LEGACY & CONNECTION

As we step into the month of September, our journey of transformative reflections continues with a profound exploration of "Legacy and Connection." Within this chapter, we embark on a path of self-discovery, embracing the power of reflection to unearth our personal legacy and reconnect with the threads that bind us to others and the world around us.

In Week 1, from September 1st to September 7th, we delve into the theme of "Reflecting on Personal Legacy: Rediscovering Our Purpose." These seven days are an invitation to pause, reflect, and contemplate the impact we wish to make on the world. Through deep introspection and contemplative practices, we unravel the layers of our being, uncovering our true purpose and the values that guide our journey. By connecting with our inner selves, we can align our actions and choices with our desired legacy, igniting a transformative path forward.

Moving into Week 2, from September 8th to September 14th, we shift our focus to "Nurturing Meaningful Connections: Cultivating Relationships that Inspire Growth." In these seven days, we explore the essence of connection and its role in our personal and collective transformation. Through meaningful interactions, heartfelt conversations, and acts of kindness, we cultivate relationships that nourish our souls and propel us toward growth. This week invites us to reflect on the connections we have and how we can deepen and expand them, forging bonds that inspire and support us on our journey.

As we enter Week 3, from September 15th to September 21st, we embrace the theme of "Embracing Interconnectedness with All Beings: Finding Unity in Diversity." In these seven days, we widen our perspective and recognize the inherent interconnectedness that binds us to all living beings. Through empathy, compassion, and a deep appreciation for diversity, we discover the beauty and strength that arise from our shared human experience. This week calls us to reflect on the ways we can foster unity, celebrate differences, and contribute to a world where all beings thrive together.

Finally, in Week 4, from September 22nd to September 30th, we honor "Ancestral Wisdom and Traditions: Embodying the Wisdom of the Past for a Transformative Future." During these seven days, we pay homage to the wisdom passed down by our ancestors, recognizing the invaluable teachings and traditions that have shaped who we are. Through reflection, storytelling, and rituals, we honor our roots and gain insights into the timeless wisdom that can guide us on our transformative journey. This week invites us to contemplate the ways we can integrate ancestral wisdom into our lives, fostering a deeper connection to our heritage and fostering growth for generations to come.

With these weekly themes, we embark on a month-long exploration of "Legacy and Connection," allowing the transformative power of reflection to guide us toward a deeper understanding of ourselves, our relationships, and our place in the world.

SEPTEMBER 1

Take a moment today to reflect on your personal legacy. What mark do you want to leave on the world? Consider the values and principles that are important to you and how they can shape your actions and decisions. Engage in a journaling exercise where you envision your ideal legacy and the steps you can take to align your life with that vision.

"Knowing yourself is the beginning of all wisdom." - Aristotle

SEPTEMBER 2

Explore the concept of personal purpose by engaging in a guided reflection exercise. Close your eyes, take a few deep breaths, and ask yourself: 'What is my true purpose in life?' Allow any thoughts or feelings to arise naturally, and without judgment, observe the insights that emerge. After the reflection, take a few moments to jot down your thoughts and any action steps that can help you live more in line with your purpose.

SEPTEMBER 3

Contemplate the people who have influenced and inspired you throughout your life. Who are the individuals that have left a lasting imprint on your journey? Take time to express gratitude for their presence and reflect on the lessons they have taught you. Consider how their influence has shaped your own values and aspirations.

SEPTEMBER 4

Engage in a mindfulness practice focused on connecting with your inner self. Find a quiet space, close your eyes, and take deep, intentional breaths. As you breathe in and out, reflect on your purpose and the core essence of who you are. What brings you joy, fulfillment, and a sense of meaning? Allow these insights to guide you in rediscovering your purpose and aligning your actions with your authentic self.

"Success is not the key to happiness. Happiness is the key to success. If you love what you are doing, you will be successful." - Albert Schweitzer

SEPTEMBER 5

Consider the lessons you have learned from past experiences and how they have shaped your personal growth. What challenges have you overcome, and how have they influenced your character? Reflect on the words of Carl Jung: 'I am not what happened to me, I am what I choose to become.' How can you use your past as a stepping stone to build a meaningful legacy?

SEPTEMBER 6

Today, engage in a conversation with a trusted friend or family member about personal legacy. Share your aspirations, dreams, and the impact you want to have on others and the world. Listen deeply to their perspective and insights. How can their feedback contribute to your journey of rediscovering your purpose? Take note of any valuable insights or perspectives that arise from this exchange.

SEPTEMBER 7

Spend time in nature and reflect on the interconnectedness of all life. As you observe the natural world around you, contemplate the ripple effect of your actions and the legacy you are creating. How can you contribute positively to the interconnected web of life? Take a moment to appreciate the beauty and harmony in nature and consider how you can align your own life with the greater tapestry of existence.

SEPTEMBER 8

Take a moment to reach out to someone who has had a positive impact on your life. Express your gratitude and appreciation for their presence. Reflect on how this person has contributed to your personal growth and consider ways you can nurture and deepen your connection with them. How can you continue to support and inspire each other on your respective journeys?

"Gratitude is not only the greatest of virtues but the parent of all others."
- Marcus Tullius Cicero

SEPTEMBER 9

Today, engage in an act of kindness towards a loved one or a stranger. Consider a small gesture that can brighten someone's day and strengthen your bond. It could be a heartfelt compliment, a listening ear, or a random act of generosity. Reflect on the ripple effect of kindness and how nurturing relationships can create a positive impact not only in our lives but also in the lives of others.

SEPTEMBER 10

Reflect on the power of empathy in building meaningful connections. Put yourself in someone else's shoes and try to understand their perspective, feelings, and experiences. How does this exercise of empathy enhance your understanding and connection with others? How can you cultivate empathy in your interactions and relationships to foster deeper understanding and mutual growth?

SEPTEMBER 11

Today, engage in active listening during your conversations. Pay close attention to the words, emotions, and nonverbal cues of the person you are speaking with. Seek to truly understand their thoughts and feelings without judgment or interruption. How does the practice of active listening deepen your connection and create a safe space for authentic communication? How can you integrate this skill into your relationships to nurture mutual growth and understanding?

SEPTEMBER 12

Reflect on the importance of vulnerability in nurturing meaningful connections. Take a moment to open up and share a personal story or struggle with someone you trust. How does vulnerability create an atmosphere of trust, authenticity, and intimacy? How can you cultivate vulnerability in your relationships to foster deeper connections and support each other's growth?

SEPTEMBER 13

Consider the role of forgiveness in nurturing meaningful connections. Reflect on any lingering resentments or grievances you hold towards others. Is there an opportunity for forgiveness and healing? How does letting go of past hurts contribute to the growth and strength of your relationships? How can you practice forgiveness to foster deeper connections and create space for growth and transformation?

SEPTEMBER 14

Today, engage in a reflective exercise where you list the qualities and values you seek in your relationships. What are the traits that inspire growth, trust, and mutual support? Reflect on how you can embody these qualities and align them with your actions and behaviors. How can you contribute to creating an environment where meaningful connections can flourish?

SEPTEMBER 15

Take a moment to observe the natural world around you. Notice the intricate web of interconnectedness that exists. Reflect on how every living being, from the smallest insect to the tallest tree, plays a vital role in the delicate balance of the ecosystem. How can you cultivate a deeper sense of interconnectedness in your own life? In what ways can you celebrate and honor the diversity of beings and recognize the unity that binds us all together?

SEPTEMBER 16

Today, engage in an act of kindness towards a stranger or someone you may not know well. It could be a simple gesture like offering a helping hand, a warm smile, or a few kind words. Reflect on the experience. How did it make you feel? How did it impact the other person? Recognize that even the smallest acts of kindness have the power to create ripples of positive change and foster a sense of interconnectedness among individuals.

"I shall pass this way but once; any good that I can do or any kindness I can show to any human being; let me do it now. Let me not defer nor neglect it, for I shall not pass this way again."
— Etienne de Grellet

SEPTEMBER 17

Take a moment to explore a different culture, whether through literature, music, art, or cuisine. Allow yourself to be curious and open-minded, embracing the diversity of human experiences. Reflect on what you can learn from different cultures and how this knowledge can deepen your understanding of interconnectedness. As Rumi once said, "You are not a drop in the ocean. You are the entire ocean in a drop." How can you embrace the richness of diversity and recognize the interconnectedness of all beings?

SEPTEMBER 18

Engage in a practice of active listening today. Choose a conversation partner and focus your attention fully on them. Listen not only to their words but also to the emotions and intentions behind them. Seek to understand rather than respond. Reflect on how this deep listening practice enhances your sense of interconnectedness with others. How does it foster empathy and create a stronger bond? Remember the words of the philosopher Epictetus: "We have two ears and one mouth so that we can listen twice as much as we speak."

SEPTEMBER 19

Spend some time in nature today and observe the intricate interdependencies between various elements. Notice how plants, animals, and even the elements themselves rely on one another for survival and growth. Reflect on the interconnectedness of ecosystems and how it mirrors our own interconnectedness as human beings. How can you extend this awareness to your daily life? In what ways can you contribute to the well-being of others and the world around you?

SEPTEMBER 20

Engage in a mindfulness practice today that emphasizes interconnectedness and unity. It could be a loving-kindness meditation where you extend well-wishes to all beings, or a gratitude practice where you acknowledge the interconnected web of support in your life. Reflect on how this practice cultivates a sense of oneness and interconnectedness. How does it shift your perspective and enhance your relationships with others?

SEPTEMBER 21

In the tapestry of life, diversity weaves a beautiful pattern of unity. Embrace the richness of our interconnected world, where differences merge to create a vibrant symphony of humanity. Reflect on the beauty that arises when diverse minds, cultures, and perspectives come together. How can you honor and celebrate the unity in diversity today? Embrace the gift of learning from others, expanding your horizons, and fostering inclusive connections. As Maya Angelou wisely said, "We all should know that diversity makes for a rich tapestry, and we must understand that all the threads of the tapestry are equal in value, no matter what their color."

SEPTEMBER 22

On this day, reflect on the rich tapestry of ancestral wisdom and traditions that have shaped your existence. Pay homage to the teachings passed down through generations, carrying the torch of wisdom into the future. How can you honor and embody the wisdom of your ancestors in your daily life? Draw inspiration from their experiences and embrace the transformative power of ancient knowledge. As Confucius wisely proclaimed, "Study the past if you would define the future."

SEPTEMBER 23

Delve into the treasure trove of your ancestral heritage and explore the customs, rituals, and practices that hold deep significance. Engage in a meaningful activity that connects you to your roots, whether it's preparing a traditional recipe, practicing a cultural dance, or learning a folk song. How does immersing yourself in your ancestral traditions nourish your sense of identity and belonging? Allow the ancient wisdom and practices to guide you on your transformative journey.

SEPTEMBER 24

As we near the end of September, let us turn our attention to the precious bonds of love and family. Love is a force that connects us, transcending barriers and nurturing our souls. Family, whether biological or chosen, provides a foundation of support, acceptance, and belonging. Reflect on the love that surrounds you and the role of family in your life. As Maya Angelou beautifully expressed, "I sustain myself with the love of family." How can you nurture and celebrate the love within your family today? Cherish the moments, embrace the connections, and let love be the guiding force that brings you closer together.

SEPTEMBER 25

Engage in a storytelling exercise to uncover the tales of your ancestors. Whether through conversations with family members or research into your genealogy, discover the stories that have shaped your family's journey. How do these stories inspire and guide you in your own life? Embrace the transformative power of storytelling and the wisdom it holds for future generations.

SEPTEMBER 26

Embark on a journey of cultural exploration and learn about the traditions and customs of other cultures. Celebrate the diversity that enriches our world and fosters unity among humanity. How does embracing cultural diversity broaden your perspective and deepen your appreciation for different traditions? As Mahatma Gandhi once said, "Our ability to reach unity in diversity will be the beauty and the test of our civilization."

SEPTEMBER 27

Reflect on the values and principles that have been passed down through your ancestral lineage. Consider the virtues and ethics that guided your predecessors and explore how they can inform your own choices and actions. How can embodying the wisdom of the past lead to a transformative future? As Nelson Mandela wisely observed, "I have walked that long road to freedom. I have tried not to falter; I have made missteps along the way. But I have discovered the secret that after climbing a great hill, one only finds that there are many more hills to climb."

SEPTEMBER 28

Engage in a ritual or ceremony that honors your ancestral traditions. It could be as simple as lighting incense, reciting a prayer, or performing a symbolic gesture. How does participating in ancestral rituals connect you to the collective wisdom of your lineage? Embrace the transformative power of rituals to bring harmony and balance into your life.

SEPTEMBER 29

On this penultimate day of September, take a moment to reflect on the transformative power of ancestral wisdom and traditions. Consider how these timeless teachings can guide you towards a more meaningful and purposeful life. In what ways can you integrate the wisdom of the past into your daily choices and actions? As Ralph Waldo Emerson once said, "What lies behind us and what lies before us are tiny matters compared to what lies within us."

SEPTEMBER 30

As we reach the final day of September, let us honor the journey we have undertaken throughout this month of reflection and connection. Take time to appreciate the growth, insights, and transformative experiences you have gained along the way. How have these reflections on personal legacy, nurturing meaningful connections, embracing interconnectedness, and honoring ancestral wisdom shaped your perspective and aspirations for the future? Embrace the wisdom gained and carry it forward into the next chapter of your transformative journey

OCTOBER – NURTURING THE MIND

As we venture into the month of October, we begin our exploration with Week 1: Cultivating Introspection and Serenity. In these first seven days, we immerse ourselves in the art of introspection, creating a sacred space for self-reflection and inner serenity. Through daily teachings and reflections, we delve into the wisdom of philosophers and contemplative practices that nourish our souls, allowing us to cultivate deeper self-awareness and find solace in the tranquility within.

Moving into Week 2: Letting Go and Embracing Change, which spans from October 8th to October 14th, we embark on a journey of releasing attachments and embracing the transformative power of change. Like the falling leaves that surrender to the wind, we explore the wisdom of philosophers who have illuminated the path of impermanence and learn to navigate life's transitions with grace and resilience. Each day presents an opportunity to reflect on what we must release and what new possibilities await us as we embrace the ever-changing nature of existence.

As we progress into Week 3: Finding Inspiration in Silence and Nature, from October 15th to October 21st, we venture into the depths of silence and reconnect with the nourishing essence of nature. Through contemplation and mindful engagement with the natural world, we uncover profound insights and rediscover our inherent interconnectedness with all living beings. In the whispers of the wind and the rustling of leaves, we find inspiration and a renewed sense of wonder.

Finally, we conclude the month with Week 4: Unveiling Inner Passions and Pursuing Aspirations, spanning from October 22nd to October 31st. In these final days, we explore the depths of our being, unearthing our inner passions and embracing the courage to pursue our aspirations. Through introspection, creative expression, and the wisdom of philosophers who dared to follow their dreams, we embark on a transformative journey of self-discovery, unmasking our true passions and stepping into a future aligned with our deepest desires.

OCTOBER 1

In the embrace of October, let us embark on a transformative journey of self-discovery. Take a moment to pause, breathe, and turn your gaze inward. In the stillness, listen closely to the whispers of your heart. What truths lie dormant within you, waiting to be unveiled? Embrace this season as an opportunity to explore the depths of your being and uncover the treasures that reside within.

OCTOBER 2

As the leaves gently fall, release the burdens that weigh upon your spirit. Reflect on what no longer serves you and consider what you can let go of in order to create space for growth. Allow the wisdom of Seneca to guide you: "It is not the man who has too little, but the man who craves more, that is poor." Embrace the freedom that comes from releasing attachments and discover the lightness that accompanies letting go.

OCTOBER 3

Amidst the quietude of October, find solace in simplicity. Socrates once said, "He who is not contented with what he has would not be contented with what he would like to have." Take a moment to reflect on the abundance that already graces your life. In this moment, what can you appreciate and be grateful for? Cultivate contentment and find joy in the simplicity of the present.

OCTOBER 4

October whispers invitations to connect with the rhythms of nature. Take a walk amidst the changing colors and allow your senses to be awakened. As Ralph Waldo Emerson wrote, "In the woods, we return to reason and faith." Embrace the beauty of the natural world and find harmony with its gentle cadence. How can you immerse yourself in nature's embrace and align with its wisdom?

OCTOBER 5

Embrace the serenity of October's stillness. Pause and observe the world with gentle curiosity. Lao Tzu reminds us, "Nature does not hurry, yet everything is accomplished." In this stillness, what can you learn about the art of patience? How can you cultivate a sense of calm amidst the chaos? Allow the tranquility of this season to nourish your soul and awaken your inner wisdom.

OCTOBER 6

Within the tranquility of October, seek the wisdom of the ancient philosophers. As Socrates once mused, "The unexamined life is not worth living." Take time for introspection and self-inquiry. Delve into the depths of your thoughts, emotions, and beliefs. What insights can you gain from looking deeply within? Embrace the power of self-reflection to illuminate your path and guide your journey.

OCTOBER 7

October invites us to cultivate gratitude for the present moment. As Marcus Aurelius said, "When you arise in the morning, think of what a precious privilege it is to be alive." Take a moment to express gratitude for something in your life today. Reflect on the blessings that surround you and appreciate the small joys that often go unnoticed. What are you thankful for in this very moment? Let gratitude fill your heart and bring a sense of profound peace and contentment.

OCTOBER 8

Amidst the barren branches and falling leaves, lies the promise of renewal. Just as nature rejuvenates itself, so too can we find the strength to let go of the old and welcome the new. Reflect on something you're holding onto that no longer serves you. How can you release it to create space for growth? Embrace the liberation that comes from shedding what no longer aligns with your authentic self.

OCTOBER 9

In the crispness of the autumn air, we can sense the ebb and flow of life's rhythms. Embrace the harmony of existence and learn to dance with the ever-changing melodies that surround us. Consider a recent change or transition in your life. How can you adapt and find harmony amidst the shifting tides? Allow yourself to flow with the currents of life, trusting that change brings new opportunities for growth.

OCTOBER 10

The chill of October whispers reminders of our mortality. Let this awareness ignite a sense of urgency to live fully, embracing each day as a precious gift and leaving a meaningful legacy behind. Reflect on what truly matters to you. How can you infuse your life with purpose and make each moment count? Embrace the present with gratitude and intention, sowing seeds that will bear fruit long after you're gone.

OCTOBER 11

Behind the veil of silence, profound truths reside. Seek the wisdom that can only be found in the depths of contemplation, for it is there that the answers to life's mysteries await. Take a moment of quietude today and reflect on a question or challenge you've been pondering. What insights arise from the depths of your contemplation? Embrace the power of introspection and allow your inner wisdom to guide you.

OCTOBER 12

Nature paints the world with hues of warmth and melancholy. Embrace the beauty of contradictions and the delicate balance between light and darkness within your own existence. Reflect on a recent experience where contrasting emotions coexisted. How can you find beauty and growth within the dance of opposites? Embrace the richness that arises from the interplay of life's contrasting shades.

OCTOBER 13

In the stillness of October nights, stars shine brightly, reminding us of the vastness of the cosmos. Allow yourself to feel small in the grand scheme of things, and let humility be your guide. Look up at the night sky and contemplate the magnitude of the universe. How does this perspective shift your perception of your own worries and concerns? Surrender to the awe-inspiring majesty of the cosmos and find solace in your place within it.

OCTOBER 14

As the winds of change sweep through October, embrace transformation as an integral part of growth. Shed the layers that no longer serve you and emerge stronger and more resilient. Reflect on a personal quality or habit that you would like to change or improve. What steps can you take to begin this transformative journey? Embrace the discomfort of growth and trust that within it lies the potential for profound personal evolution.

OCTOBER 15

Amidst the autumn's embrace, find solace in the silence that surrounds you. Embrace moments of stillness and allow them to awaken your senses. As Albert Einstein once said, "I think 99 times and find nothing. I stop thinking, swim in silence, and the truth comes to me." How can you attune yourself to the harmony of the universe today? Embrace the power of silence and allow it to reveal profound insights and truths.

OCTOBER 16

October invites us to cultivate gratitude for the present moment. Take a moment to express gratitude for something in your life today. Reflect on the blessings that surround you and appreciate the small joys that often go unnoticed. What are you thankful for in this very moment? Let gratitude fill your heart and bring a sense of profound peace and contentment.

OCTOBER 17

In the gentle rustling of leaves and the whispers of the wind, nature offers its wisdom to those who listen. Take a moment to immerse yourself in the sounds of nature and connect with the rhythms of life. What lessons can you learn from the natural world around you today? Listen closely to the wisdom that nature whispers, for it holds profound insights into the cycles of life, growth, and renewal.

OCTOBER 18

October invites us to step outside the boundaries of routine and explore the wonders of the natural world. Venture into nature and allow its vastness to expand your perspective. As John Muir proclaimed, "In every walk with nature, one receives far more than he seeks." What revelations await you on your next journey into the great outdoors? Embrace the sense of awe and wonder that nature inspires and let it open your mind to new possibilities.

OCTOBER 19

Within the simplicity of nature's design lies profound elegance. Embrace minimalism and let go of excess to find clarity and tranquility. Reflect on an area of your life that could benefit from simplification. How can you create more space for what truly matters? Just as nature thrives with its simple yet essential elements, so too can you find greater fulfillment by focusing on what is truly meaningful and essential in your own life.

OCTOBER 20

October's serenity beckons us to engage in acts of mindful presence. Embrace the present moment fully and immerse yourself in the beauty that surrounds you. As Thich Nhat Hanh teaches, "The present moment is filled with joy and happiness. If you are attentive, you will see it." How can you cultivate greater mindfulness in your daily life? Let go of distractions and embrace the richness of the present moment, allowing it to unfold with all its beauty and potential.

OCTOBER 21

Amidst October's tapestry of transformation, find inspiration in the cycles of life. Witness the withering leaves that give way to new growth, and reflect on the seasons of change within your own journey. Consider a recent experience of personal growth or transformation. What can you learn from this process of change? Embrace the wisdom of nature's cycles and trust in the transformative power of embracing life's inevitable transitions.

OCTOBER 22

As October nears its end, let us reflect on the power of human connection. Reach out to someone you care about and express gratitude for their presence in your life. As Aristotle once said, "Friendship is a single soul dwelling in two bodies." How can you nurture and deepen your relationships today?

OCTOBER 23

In the spirit of October's communal harvest, recognize the strength that lies in unity and collaboration. Seek opportunities to work together and harness the collective wisdom and talents of those around you. Reflect on a recent experience where teamwork brought about positive outcomes. How can you foster collaboration in your personal and professional life?

OCTOBER 24

October invites us to cultivate empathy and compassion for others. Take a moment to put yourself in someone else's shoes and consider their perspective. As Confucius wisely said, "Do not do to others what you do not want done to yourself." How can you extend kindness and understanding to those around you?

OCTOBER 25

Within the tapestry of diverse perspectives lies the richness of human experience. Embrace the beauty of differences and engage in meaningful conversations that broaden your horizons. Reflect on a belief or viewpoint that differs from your own. How can you approach this difference with curiosity and respect?

OCTOBER 26

Amidst the darkness of October nights, let kindness be your guiding light. Extend a helping hand or perform an act of service for someone in need. As Mahatma Gandhi said, "The best way to find yourself is to lose yourself in the service of others." How can you make a positive impact in someone's life today?

OCTOBER 27

October's twilight invites us to gather around the metaphorical hearth and share stories that connect us. Take time to listen deeply to the narratives of others and honor the wisdom they impart. Reflect on a personal story or experience that has shaped you. What lessons can you learn from your own narrative?

OCTOBER 28

Within the embrace of October's community, find gratitude for the support and love that surrounds you. Express appreciation to those who have made a difference in your life. Reflect on the impact that community has had on your personal growth. How can you contribute to creating a supportive and nurturing community?

OCTOBER 29

As October transitions into its final days, take a moment to reflect on the passage of time and the impermanence of all things. Embrace the wisdom of Heraclitus, who said, "You cannot step into the same river twice." How can you find peace and acceptance in the ever-changing nature of life?

OCTOBER 30

In the last moments of October, let us honor the lessons learned and the growth experienced throughout the month. Take time to journal or reflect on the insights gained, the challenges overcome, and the moments of joy and gratitude. How has October shaped your perspective and inspired your journey?

OCTOBER 31

As the month bids farewell, October's spirit lingers in the air. Embrace the magic and mystery of this transition and welcome the opportunities that lie ahead. Reflect on a personal intention or goal for the coming months. How can you carry the wisdom and inspiration of October forward into your pursuit of passions and aspirations?

NOVEMBER – GRATITUDE AND RESILIENCE

As the crisp air embraces the world, November ushers in the spirit of gratitude and resilience. It is a month that symbolizes the changing seasons and reminds us of the importance of embracing gratitude and inner strength as we prepare for the approaching winter. In this chapter of transformative reflections, we will delve into the profound themes of cultivating gratitude, nurturing resilience, seeking wisdom through reflection and mindfulness, and embracing unity and compassion in relationships.

Week 1: Cultivating Gratitude and Thankfulness

In the first week of November, we embark on a journey of cultivating gratitude and thankfulness. It is a time to pause, reflect, and appreciate the abundance of blessings in our lives. Through practices of gratitude, we can shift our focus from scarcity to abundance, finding joy in the simple moments and expressing gratitude for all that enriches our lives. By cultivating gratitude and thankfulness, we open ourselves to a deeper sense of contentment and happiness.

Week 2: Nurturing Resilience in Times of Adversity

As the second week unfolds, we turn our attention to nurturing resilience in times of adversity. November presents us with an opportunity to strengthen our inner resolve, embrace challenges, and rise above difficulties. We will explore strategies to cultivate resilience, draw inspiration from stories of resilience and triumph, and reflect on our own inner sources of strength. By nurturing resilience, we can navigate life's obstacles with courage, perseverance, and a greater sense of empowerment.

Week 3: Seeking Wisdom through Reflection and Mindfulness

In the third week of November, we embark on a journey of seeking wisdom through reflection and mindfulness. This is a time to slow down, create space for introspection, and cultivate a deeper connection with ourselves. Through practices of reflection and mindfulness, we gain clarity, discover inner truths, and tap into our innate wisdom. By embracing the power of reflection and mindfulness, we can navigate life's complexities with greater presence, authenticity, and inner peace.

Week 4: Embracing Unity and Compassion in Relationships

As November draws to a close and winter approaches, we shift our focus to embracing unity and compassion in relationships. It is a time to recognize our interconnectedness with others and foster deeper connections based on empathy, kindness, and understanding. We will explore the power of compassion in our relationships and reflect on ways to cultivate unity, harmony, and a sense of belonging. By embracing unity and compassion, we create a ripple effect of positive change, transforming not only our relationships but also the world around us.

In this month of November, as nature transitions to winter's embrace, we invite you to embark on a transformative journey of gratitude and resilience. Through the exploration of these themes, may you deepen your sense of appreciation, nurture your inner strength, cultivate wisdom, and foster compassion in your relationships. May this journey awaken within you a profound sense of gratitude for the richness of life and empower you to navigate life's challenges with resilience, wisdom, and an open heart.

NOVEMBER 1

Take a moment today to reflect on the abundance in your life. Consider the simple pleasures, the relationships that bring you joy, and the opportunities that have come your way. Write down three things you are grateful for and why they bring you happiness. How does recognizing abundance enhance your overall well-being?

NOVEMBER 2

Start a gratitude journal today. Each day, write down three things you are grateful for. They can be big or small, specific or general. Take a few moments to reflect on these blessings and express your gratitude. How does the act of gratitude journaling shift your perspective and bring more positivity into your day?

NOVEMBER 3

Engage in acts of kindness today. Whether it's a simple gesture like holding the door for someone or a more significant act of service, spread kindness and compassion wherever you go. Notice how these acts of kindness not only impact others but also bring a sense of fulfillment and gratitude into your own life. How can you make kindness a regular part of your daily interactions?

"Kindness is a language which the deaf can hear and the blind can see." - Mark Twain

NOVEMBER 4

Go for a walk in nature today and allow yourself to fully immerse in the beauty around you. As you stroll through the landscape, take note of the colors, the sounds, and the scents. Practice gratitude by expressing appreciation for the natural world and all its wonders. How does connecting with nature deepen your sense of gratitude and inspire feelings of awe and wonder?

NOVEMBER 5

Engage in a gratitude meditation today. Find a quiet and comfortable space, close your eyes, and focus on your breath. With each inhale and exhale, bring to mind things you are grateful for. Allow feelings of gratitude to fill your heart and radiate throughout your body. How does a gratitude meditation enhance your sense of well-being and bring a greater sense of peace and contentment?

NOVEMBER 6

Take time today to express gratitude for the meaningful relationships in your life. Reach out to a loved one and let them know how much you appreciate them. Reflect on the ways in which these relationships enrich your life and bring you joy. How can you nurture and cultivate these connections to foster even deeper bonds of love and gratitude?

"Gratitude unlocks the fullness of life. It turns what we have into enough, and more. It turns denial into acceptance, chaos into order, confusion into clarity... Gratitude makes sense of our past, brings peace for today, and creates a vision for tomorrow." - Melody Beattie

NOVEMBER 7

Amidst the crisp autumn air of November, let gratitude be the flame that illuminates your path. Take a moment to reflect on the blessings in your life and express your gratitude for them. Reach out to someone you appreciate and let them know how much they mean to you. As Marcel Proust once wrote, "Let us be grateful to the people who make us happy; they are the charming gardeners who make our souls blossom." How can you cultivate a spirit of gratitude today and spread its warmth to those around you?

NOVEMBER 8

Amidst the storms of life, find solace in the power of resilience. Take a moment to reflect on a past experience where you faced adversity and emerged stronger. What qualities within you allowed you to overcome the challenge? How can you draw upon those strengths in your current situation?

NOVEMBER 9

In the face of adversity, nourish your resilience with self-care. Take time for activities that replenish your energy and bring you joy. Engage in a practice that nurtures your well-being, whether it's meditation, exercise, or indulging in a hobby. As Audre Lorde reminds us, "Caring for myself is not self-indulgence, it is self-preservation, and that is an act of political warfare." How can you prioritize self-care and strengthen your resilience from within?

NOVEMBER 10

Resilience flourishes when we adopt a growth mindset. Embrace the belief that challenges and setbacks are opportunities for growth and learning. Reflect on a recent setback or failure and identify the lessons it offered you. How can you reframe your perspective and see adversity as a catalyst for personal development? Recall the words of Winston Churchill, "Success is not final, failure is not fatal: It is the courage to continue that counts." Cultivate a growth mindset and let resilience bloom.

NOVEMBER 11

During tough times, seek inspiration from stories of resilience. Read about individuals who have overcome adversity and draw strength from their experiences. Reflect on a story that resonates with you and write down the lessons you can apply to your own life. As Helen Keller once said, "Character cannot be developed in ease and quiet. Only through experience of trial and suffering can the soul be strengthened, ambition inspired, and success achieved." Let the stories of resilience ignite a fire of determination within you.

NOVEMBER 12

In the midst of November's transformative winds, let kindness be the steady beacon that guides your way. Embrace the challenges and uncertainties with a resilient spirit, and find strength in nurturing meaningful connections. As Maya Angelou once said, "I've learned that people will forget what you said, people will forget what you did, but people will never forget how you made them feel." How can you make a positive impact in someone's life today? Embrace the opportunity to extend compassion, lend a listening ear, or offer a helping hand. Even amidst the winds of change, let your acts of kindness create warmth and inspire resilience in those around you.

NOVEMBER 13

Resilience is nourished by embracing a positive mindset. Shift your focus to the blessings and opportunities that exist even amidst adversity. Take a moment to write down three things you are grateful for in your life right now. How can you cultivate a sense of positivity and optimism in the face of challenges? Remember the words of Viktor Frankl, "Everything can be taken from a man but one thing: the last of the human freedoms—to choose one's attitude in any given set of circumstances." Choose resilience, choose positivity.

NOVEMBER 14

In the journey of resilience, it is essential to practice self-compassion. During difficult times, it is important to be gentle with yourself and acknowledge that setbacks are a natural part of the human experience. Amidst the challenges you face, take a moment to offer yourself words of kindness and understanding. Nurture a compassionate relationship with yourself, acknowledging your strengths and accepting your vulnerabilities. How can you cultivate self-compassion in your life? Embrace the practice of self-care, treat yourself with patience and forgiveness, and allow yourself the space to heal and grow. Remember the wisdom of Buddha, who said, "You yourself, as much as anybody in the entire universe, deserve your love and affection."

NOVEMBER 15

Amidst the tranquility of November's embrace, find solace in the power of stillness. Take a moment to quiet your mind and allow the present moment to unfold before you. Embrace the wisdom of Eckhart Tolle, who reminds us, "Realize deeply that the present moment is all you have. Make the NOW the primary focus of your life." How can you cultivate a sense of presence and mindfulness today? Allow yourself to fully immerse in the richness of each passing moment.

NOVEMBER 16

Amidst the rich tapestry of November's colors, immerse yourself in the beauty of nature and embrace the wisdom it holds. Take a walk through the crisp autumn air, observing the changing leaves and the gentle dance of the wind. Reflect on the cycles of nature and the lessons they impart. As you witness the transition from vibrant hues to the bare branches, contemplate the impermanence of life and the importance of embracing change. Draw inspiration from the words of Henry David Thoreau, who said, "Live in each season as it passes; breathe the air, drink the drink, taste the fruit, and resign yourself to the influence of each." How can you embrace the wisdom of nature's cycles in your own journey of self-reflection?

NOVEMBER 17

In the silence of your surroundings, listen closely to the whispers of your inner wisdom. Create space for introspection and self-reflection. As Friedrich Nietzsche once said, "He who has a why to live can bear almost any how." Take a moment to reflect on your values, beliefs, and goals. What insights can you gain from this process of self-examination? Embrace the opportunity to deepen your understanding of yourself and align your actions with your authentic self.

NOVEMBER 18

November invites you to embark on a journey of seeking wisdom through reflection and mindfulness. Embrace the power of introspection and deepen your understanding of yourself and the world around you. Set aside moments of stillness to quiet the noise of daily life and allow your inner wisdom to emerge. As Lao Tzu wisely said, "Knowing others is intelligence; knowing yourself is true wisdom. Mastering others is strength; mastering yourself is true power." Reflect on these words and contemplate how you can integrate reflection and mindfulness into your daily life. How can you deepen your self-awareness and cultivate wisdom through the practice of reflection and mindfulness?

NOVEMBER 19

Amidst the chaos of daily life, find moments of stillness and solitude. Carve out time for contemplation and introspection. As you delve into the depths of your inner being, reflect on your dreams, aspirations, and the desires of your heart. What insights can you glean from this journey within? Draw inspiration from the words of Rumi, who said, "The quieter you become, the more you are able to hear." How can you create space for silence and reflection in your life?

NOVEMBER 20

Within the pages of a book or the lines of poetry, seek wisdom and inspiration. Engage in reading materials that provoke thought, challenge your perspectives, and nourish your soul. As you immerse yourself in the words of great thinkers, allow their wisdom to guide you on your own journey of self-discovery. Reflect on a book or passage that has deeply impacted you. How can you integrate the lessons and insights gained from reading into your daily life?

NOVEMBER 21

In the journey of seeking wisdom through reflection and mindfulness, today we delve into the practice of cultivating mindful awareness. Mindfulness allows us to fully experience the present moment and deepen our understanding of ourselves and the world. Today, engage in a mindfulness exercise that helps anchor your awareness in the present.

Take a walk outdoors, allowing yourself to be fully present in each step. Pay attention to the sensation of your feet touching the ground, the rhythm of your breath, and the sights and sounds around you. As you walk, bring your attention to the present moment, observing without judgment. Notice the sensations in your body, the movement of your muscles, and the shifting of your weight with each step.

As you walk mindfully, let go of distractions and worries. Instead, focus on the simple act of walking and immerse yourself in the experience. With each step, cultivate a sense of gratitude for the ability to move, breathe, and witness the world around you.

Reflection: How does mindful walking help you connect with the present moment? What insights or sensations arise as you immerse yourself in the act of walking mindfully? How can you integrate this practice of mindful awareness into other aspects of your life?

Remember, the practice of mindfulness is an ongoing journey. Embrace each step with curiosity and compassion as you deepen your connection to yourself and the world through the power of present-moment awareness.

NOVEMBER 22

Today, let us immerse ourselves in the practice of cultivating empathy. Take a moment to step into the shoes of others and view the world from their perspective. Listen attentively, without judgment, to their stories, experiences, and emotions. By cultivating empathy, we deepen our understanding and forge genuine connections with others. Reflect on the words of Brené Brown, who said, "Empathy is a choice, and it's a vulnerable choice because in order to connect with you, I have to connect with something in myself that knows that feeling." How can you foster empathy in your relationships today?

NOVEMBER 23

In the spirit of unity and compassion, today is an invitation to perform acts of kindness for others. Engage in small gestures that can brighten someone's day, whether it's a kind word, a supportive action, or a thoughtful gesture. As Aesop once said, "No act of kindness, no matter how small, is ever wasted." Reflect on the impact of your acts of kindness and consider how you can continue to spread compassion in your daily interactions.

NOVEMBER 24

In the journey of personal growth and cultivating compassion, forgiveness plays a pivotal role. Today, take a moment to reflect on any resentments or grudges that you may be holding onto, and explore the transformative power of forgiveness.

Find a comfortable and quiet space where you can sit undisturbed. Close your eyes and take a few deep breaths, allowing yourself to relax and settle into the present moment.

Bring to mind a person or situation that has caused you pain or hurt. Allow yourself to fully acknowledge and feel the emotions that arise.

Recognize that holding onto resentment only perpetuates your own suffering. Shift your focus to the intention of forgiveness, understanding that it is a gift you give yourself.

Repeat the following affirmations silently or out loud:

"I acknowledge the pain I have experienced."
"I release my attachment to anger and resentment."
"I choose to cultivate forgiveness and compassion."
"I forgive [name of person or situation] and release them from any negative hold over me."
"I wish them well and send them love."

As you repeat these affirmations, visualize yourself letting go of the negative emotions and feel a sense of lightness and relief in your heart.

Take a few moments to rest in this space of forgiveness and compassion, allowing yourself to experience the liberation it brings.

When you are ready, gently open your eyes and carry this sense of forgiveness and liberation with you throughout your day.

Remember, forgiveness is a journey that takes time and practice. Be patient and kind to yourself as you navigate this process. By cultivating forgiveness, you create space for healing, growth, and deeper connections in your relationships.

NOVEMBER 25

Today, practice the art of compassionate listening. Create a safe space for someone to express themselves fully, without interruption or judgment. Truly listen to their words, feelings, and needs with an open heart and mind. Compassionate listening allows us to honor the experiences of others, deepen our connection, and offer support and understanding. Reflect on the words of Thich Nhat Hanh, who said, "Deep listening is the kind of listening that can help relieve the suffering of another person." How can you practice compassionate listening today and nurture more meaningful connections?

NOVEMBER 26

Express gratitude for the relationships in your life today. Take a moment to reflect on the people who bring joy, love, and support into your world. Write a heartfelt message of gratitude or reach out to them to let them know how much they mean to you. As you cultivate gratitude for the relationships you cherish, you deepen the bonds of connection and appreciation. Reflect on the ways in which these relationships have enriched your life and consider how you can nurture them further.

NOVEMBER 27

Today, take a moment to reflect on the profound power of unity and the interconnectedness of all beings. Consider the events that have unfolded in the world, where people from different backgrounds and cultures have come together for a common purpose.

One such example is the global response to natural disasters. When hurricanes, earthquakes, or other calamities strike, people from all walks of life unite to provide support, aid, and relief. In those moments, borders and differences fade away as humanity extends a helping hand to those in need.

Consider how you can contribute to unity in your own life and communities. It can be as simple as fostering understanding, promoting inclusivity, or engaging in acts of service. Each small action has the potential to create a ripple effect of positive change.

Embracing unity and interconnectedness allows us to build a more compassionate and resilient world. Let this awareness guide your actions and inspire you to create connections, extend compassion, and foster understanding among all beings.

NOVEMBER 28

On this day, immerse yourself fully in the present moment and embrace gratitude for the here and now. Release worries about the past or future, and instead, focus on the beauty and blessings that surround you in this very moment.

Reflect on the simple joys that often go unnoticed—the warmth of sunlight, the sound of laughter, or the taste of a delicious meal. Cultivate a deep sense of appreciation for the present moment and the abundance it holds.

Allow gratitude to fill your heart as you recognize the preciousness of each passing moment. Embrace the practice of mindfulness to anchor yourself in the present and experience the richness of life unfolding before you.

NOVEMBER 29

As November nears its end, take time to reflect on the lessons and growth you have experienced throughout the month. Consider the challenges faced, the resilience cultivated, and the moments of gratitude that have shaped your journey.

Reflect on the wisdom gained through introspection, mindfulness, and the teachings of great thinkers. Acknowledge the progress made on your path of personal growth and celebrate the resilience that has carried you through.

Take this opportunity to express gratitude for the lessons learned, even those wrapped in hardship. Each experience has contributed to your growth, resilience, and wisdom.

NOVEMBER 30

On this final day of November, welcome the dawn of a new month with a sense of anticipation and openness. Embrace the transition and see it as an opportunity for renewal, growth, and continued exploration.

Take a moment to set intentions for the coming month, reflecting on the gratitude and resilience cultivated in November. Consider how you can carry these qualities forward and incorporate them into the days ahead.

Embrace the unknown possibilities that lie before you, trusting in your ability to navigate whatever challenges or joys may come your way. Welcome the new month with a spirit of optimism, gratitude, and a commitment to personal growth.

As November concludes, let the gratitude and resilience cultivated during this month serve as a foundation for the journey ahead. Embrace the transformative power of reflection, mindfulness, and the pursuit of wisdom as you step into the next chapter of your life.

Welcome, December, with open arms and a heart filled with gratitude, resilience, and a deep appreciation for the beauty of each passing moment.

EMBRACING THE WISDOM OF AUTUMN'S TRANSFORMATIVE REFLECTIONS

As we reach the end of our journey through the transformative months of September, October, and November, we emerge with a deeper understanding of ourselves, the world around us, and the power of reflection. Autumn's embrace has guided us through themes of legacy, connection, nurturing the mind, and cultivating gratitude and resilience, leaving us transformed and inspired.

Throughout this book, we have explored the beauty and significance of legacy, recognizing that our actions today shape the legacy we leave behind. We have forged meaningful connections, understanding the profound impact of human relationships and the interconnectedness of all beings. Nurturing the mind has become a daily practice, as we expand our intellectual horizons and cultivate a fertile landscape of thoughts and ideas. Gratitude and resilience have become our guiding lights, illuminating the path even in the face of adversity.

As we conclude this book, let us carry the wisdom of autumn's transformative reflections with us. Let us embrace the lessons learned, the insights gained, and the practices cultivated. May the legacy we create be one of compassion, love, and positive impact. May our connections with others be authentic, nurturing, and supportive. May our minds continue to grow and flourish, embracing knowledge and wisdom. And may gratitude and resilience be our constant companions, empowering us to face life's challenges with grace and strength.

Remember, reflection is not confined to a specific season or time. It is a lifelong journey, a continuous invitation to deepen our self-awareness, nourish our minds, and cultivate gratitude and resilience. Let the transformative reflections we have explored in this book serve as a foundation for further growth and self-discovery.

As you embark on the next chapters of your personal journey, may you carry the spirit of autumn's transformative reflections with you. May you find solace in the changing seasons, inspiration in the beauty of nature, and wisdom in the depths of your own reflections. May each day be an opportunity to embrace personal growth, connect with others, and contribute to the betterment of our world.

Thank you for joining us on this transformative autumn voyage. May the wisdom gained within these pages continue to guide and inspire you as you embrace the transformative power of reflection in your everyday life.

A GLIMPSE OF THE JOURNEY AHEAD

As we conclude our exploration of transformative reflections in the autumn season, we find ourselves at a juncture where we can glimpse the journey that lies ahead. While our current book has offered insights into legacy, connection, nurturing the mind, and gratitude, there is still much wisdom to uncover in the forthcoming volumes of the "Daily Reflections for Personal Growth" series.

In Book 2, "Winter - Embracing Stillness," we will immerse ourselves in the serene embrace of the winter season. It is a time of hushed whispers and tranquil landscapes, inviting us to delve deep into the realm of introspection and self-discovery. We will find solace in the art of stillness, allowing us to reflect upon the paths we have traversed and the transformations that await us. With each passing page, we will embark on a transformative journey that will guide us towards new beginnings and set the stage for profound personal growth.

Within the pages of Book 2, we will explore the themes of reflection and stillness in December, where we will delve into the power of introspection and the transformative potential that lies within moments of deep contemplation. In January, we will embark on a path of self-discovery, navigating the uncharted territories of our inner landscapes and unearthing the dormant seeds of our true selves. And as we reach February, the month of serenity and mindfulness, we will learn to embrace the present moment fully, nurturing our capacity for awareness and finding peace in the simplicity of being.

With each turn of the page, we will delve deeper into the depths of winter's wisdom, uncovering insights that will guide us towards personal growth and transformation. The journey ahead promises to be one of profound introspection and discovery, inviting us to embrace the stillness within and kindle the flames of our innermost desires.

So, as we bid farewell to this book and the autumn season, let us eagerly anticipate the arrival of winter and the revelations it holds. May the pages that follow in Book 2 of the "Daily Reflections for Personal Growth" series envelop us in the serenity of stillness, as we embark on a journey of self-exploration and embrace the transformative power of winter's embrace.

ABOUT THE AUTHOR

In lands of rich cultural hue,
A seeker of wisdom once grew.
Nurtured in the Netherlands' embrace,
Their journey began with youthful grace.

Through academic corridors they roamed,
Mastery of business and management honed.
Immersed in knowledge's profound call,
Crafting a tapestry, standing tall.

Venturing far, to lands unknown,
Embracing diverse cultures, seeds sown.
From Netherlands' streets to Singapore's domain,
Communication's webs they'd deftly tame.

In philosophy's depths, their heart found fire,
Critical thinking and truth their desire.
Layers of human nature they unveil,
Inviting readers on a transformative trail.

In daily reflections, a sacred dance,
Nourishing minds with wisdom's chance.
An invitation to seek and explore,
Enlightenment's path forevermore.

So, let us embark on this poetic flight,
Guided by their words, shining bright.
In the author's embrace, we find our way,
Through daily reflections, come what may.